Brief Notes

INSURANCE AND RISK MANAGEMENT

The publications in *Brief Notes* are outlines of core topics of interest to professionals involved in shopping center management. The outlines are capsule overviews of each topic. Many key points are covered, and shopping center examples are provided for further illustration. Core concepts in each area guide you on topics you may want to explore further. Each outline also contains a helpful glossary.

Brief Notes is designed to provide a helpful and informative overview of the topics covered. It is not intended to be a substitute for more extensive learning that can be achieved through attending ICSC educational programs and reading additional ICSC professional publications.

The outlines contained in *Brief Notes: Shopping Center Management:*

- Management Overview
- Finance
- Insurance and Risk Management
- The Lease and Its Language
- Leasing Strategies
- Maintenance
- Marketing
- Retailing
- Security

Brief Notes

INSURANCE AND RISK MANAGEMENT

International Council of Shopping Centers
New York

ABOUT THE INTERNATIONAL COUNCIL OF SHOPPING CENTERS

The International Council of Shopping Centers (ICSC) is the trade association of the shopping center industry. Serving the shopping center industry since 1957, ICSC is a not-for-profit organization with over 44,000 members in 77 countries worldwide.

ICSC members include shopping center

- owners
- developers
- managers
- marketing specialists
- leasing agents
- retailers
- researchers
- attorneys
- architects
- contractors
- consultants
- investors
- lenders and brokers
- academics
- public officials

ICSC sponsors more than 200 meetings a year and provides a wide array of services and products for shopping center professionals, including deal making events, conferences, educational programs, accreditation, awards, publications and research data.

For more information about ICSC, write or call the
International Council of Shopping Centers
1221 Avenue of the Americas
New York, NY 10020-1099
Telephone: 646-728-3800
Fax: 212-589-5555
info@icsc.org
http://www.icsc.org

Companies, professional groups, clubs and other organizations may qualify for special terms when ordering quantities of more than 20 of this title.

Published by
International Council of Shopping Centers
Publications Department
1221 Avenue of the Americas
New York, NY 10020-1099

ICSC Catalog No.: 242

ISBN: 1-58268-028-0

Contents

Preface

Insurance is a contract between a risk-taker (the insurer) and another party (the insured) in which, for a fee (the premium), the insurer agrees to pay the insured for losses to something specific (the risk) due to named causes (hazards or perils). The insurer may also assume the obligation to pay a third party (the claimant) on behalf of the insured.

Insurance is also a major expense to shopping center owners and tenants. Risk management is the key to controlling that expense.

Buyers of insurance shouldn't rely solely on agents and brokers, but should themselves be involved, and that means (1) having a good understanding of what insurance is all about and (2) understanding the ways to transfer risk.

The task is not as formidable as it seems. The following pages explain the key points that will help you—the shopping center professional—to understand both insurance policies and those parts of a lease that deal with property damage and liability.

Acknowledgments

The material in this outline is based in part on a course presented at the International Council of Shopping Centers (ICSC) John T. Riordan School for Professional Development Management Institute.

The International Council of Shopping Centers gratefully acknowledges the individuals mentioned below, who have contributed their expertise to this publication.

Robert G. Nelson, Partner, Nelson & Bernstein LLC
Donald P. Pipino, CPCU, Chairman Emeritus, Gallagher Pipino, Inc.

Core Concepts

✓ Limit exposure

✓ Transfer risk

✓ Know your coverage

MANAGING RISKS

Identifying Risks

Risk is the chance you take of incurring a loss, and insurance is one method you can use for sharing that risk. When you take out an insurance policy, you transfer risk to a professional risk bearer—the insurance company.

There are two kinds of risk:

- Business: These are entrepreneurial risks and cannot be insured against. You cannot, for example, insure against not making your sales projections or people not coming to your newly opened center.

- Static, or nonbusiness: These are external hazards, and they *can* be insured against. They include, for example, flood, fire and slips and falls.

How to Manage Risk Successfully

The risk management process is a common sense approach to handling risk and is an integral part of a daily management program.

The most obvious way to avoid risks is to never let them occur in the first place. Other possibilities are:

- To monitor the design and selection of building materials for your center
- To refrain from renting to the type of tenant who may present a danger to your kind of center.

To know what risks you are running:

- Use a checklist specifically designed for your center to help you identify risks such as trip and fall hazards and faulty wiring.
- Be aware of any environmental hazards, such as asbestos or mold, that may be present at your center.

Eliminate or Minimize Risks

Once a risk has been identified, do everything possible to eliminate it. For example:

- Have an ongoing maintenance program to eliminate hazards, such as cracks in sidewalks, once they have been discovered.

If a risk cannot be eliminated, try to minimize it. The risk of fire cannot be eliminated, but the installation of fire extinguishers can mean a 90% reduction of exposure to fire.

Even after avoiding and eliminating risks, your center may still be exposed to loss. You can assume these unavoidable risks yourself. Be sure to base decisions to assume risk on good hard facts, including:

- Identifying unavoidable risks (fire, for example)
- Determining how much risk you can economically pay for yourself, so that you can set realistic deductibles.

Transfer Risks

You need not always assume unavoidable risks yourself. You may let someone else take them on. You can do this by using the following methods.

- Noninsurance: This involves transferring risk to others and includes the use of leases, which transfer risks to tenants. Other options include contracts and agreements with contractors, vendors and people running special events at your center that make them liable for risks.
- Insurance: This allows you to transfer risk to a professional risk bearer—an insurance carrier.

Monitor Your Coverage

The insurance industry is dynamic and constantly changing both policies and rates. Following 9/11, rates and premiums began escalating dramatically while some coverages were being eliminated, such as terrorism. Be alert for changes that may occur in the following areas:

- The law
- Obligations you have to the public and to your tenants
- Environmental responsibilities
- Coverage provided by your policies. (For example, in 1986 insurers quietly eliminated coverage for all kinds of environmental pollution.)

Core Concepts

✓ Policy is a contract

✓ Know key terms

✓ What is not covered

THE INSURANCE POLICY

Virtually every insurance policy is divided into specific sections that include:

- Declaration: The page on the front of the policy is the housekeeping part of the policy. It identifies the policy as yours and may set out the limits and describe the coverage that the policy provides.
- Insuring agreement: This says, in fairly explicit terms, just what the policy is for—for example, that it insures against all risk of physical loss or, in the case of a liability policy, that it protects you against claims for bodily injury or property damage.
- Definitions: This section defines the terms used in the pol-

icy. It may specify, for example, something as simple as the name of the person or company that is insured or something as complicated as what is meant when the policy insures you against an "occurrence."

- Exclusions: This section defines the items that are not covered by the policy. Often, items are excluded because they are meant to be covered by another kind of policy. For example, fire and theft insurance will exclude losses arising out of the acts of a dishonest employee because a fidelity bond will cover those acts.
- Conditions: This is the part of a policy that lays down the ground rules. For example, it may include:

  —How the policy is audited
  —When you have to present a claim
  —To whom you should present a claim
  —How timely you must be in presenting a claim
  —What you have to do to protect the damaged property in the event of a loss
  —When you can sue the insurance company
  —What you must do before you sue the insurance company in case there is a dispute regarding a claim.

Core Concepts

- ✓ Building, personal property, income, improvements
- ✓ Perils
- ✓ Replacement vs. actual cash value
- ✓ Conditions
- ✓ Hazards

PROPERTY INSURANCE

Property insurance covers the insured for damages to his or her personal or real property or the loss of its use. It is a first-party insurance. Property is defined by the individual policy.

There is no such thing as a standard policy; even among the largest companies, policies may differ. In order to understanding what it is that is insured, and by whom, you must understand what is written in your specific policy.

Know What Is Insured

Careful analysis will give you a clear understanding of what is meant by the following terms:

- Building: This generally includes any kind of permanently installed fixture, all building materials and janitorial equipment. Check to see what other things are part of the building definition. Consider, for example, freestanding signs, retaining walls, parking lots, wall-to-wall carpeting and drapes.
- Rental income: Coverage for loss of rents usually begins when a building is destroyed, but it may end when the building is ready for reoccupancy. (For a small premium you may extend coverage up to six months or until released.)
- Business income and extra expense. This coverage is for loss of profits and for continuing expenses for operations other than property rental.
- Personal property: This coverage basically revolves around furniture, fixtures and office equipment. Here the problem is more likely to center around the amount of coverage you have rather than its definitions. Remember that in the event of loss, this material will have to be replaced, and the cost may prove significant.
- Tenant's improvements: They may become the landlord's property (a) when the lease expires, (b) as soon as they are permanently attached or (c) at some other stipulated time. The lease will tell you who is supposed to insure tenant's improvements.

Know How to Insure the Property

Special causes of loss insurance protects the insured from all perils and causes *except* those specifically excluded.

Perils are inherent things, such as windstorms or explosions, that can cause a loss or injury. When such a loss occurs, its cause must be identified to determine if coverage applies.

Special causes of loss coverage has generally replaced that for fire, extended coverage and vandalism. It should always be used in leases to describe the coverage to be carried by the lessee.

Know How to Value What You Are Insuring

When property is destroyed, you have two options: (1) to replace it or (2) to have the carrier pay you the destroyed property's actual cash value. Property may be insured in either of these two ways. In either case, appraisal services are useful in determining the amount you should insure.

1. Replacement cost: This can be determined by taking the amount it originally cost to build the building and adding it to today's increased cost of construction. It is often used when insuring buildings less than five years old. If original costs are unknown or the building is older than five years, a replacement cost appraisal may be secured.
2. Actual cash value: This is meant to be the cost of replacing a building in today's market, less depreciation. It may be used, for example, if you know in advance that you would not want to replace a building should it be destroyed.

Insuring to Value

Because most losses are partial losses, it is to the insurance company's advantage to have you insure to value. To encourage you to do this, insurers reduce the rate as you go up from 70% to 80% to 90% to 100% (full value and the lowest rate they offer). To prevent people from saying they were insuring for 100% when in reality they were insuring for only half the value of the property, insurance companies use a coinsurance clause.

- Coinsurance clause: At the time of loss, this allows the insurance company to evaluate the replacement cost of the property. If the insurance company finds that you claimed you were insuring to 100% of value but had in truth only insured to 50% of value, they will pay only 50% or a partial loss. For example, if a building were worth $10,000,000 and you only carried $5,000,000, the loss payment on a $1,000,000 loss would be

$$\frac{\text{Amt Carried} \quad 5{,}000{,}000}{\text{Amt Required} \quad 10{,}000{,}000} = 50\% \times$$

$$\text{Amount of Loss } \$1{,}000{,}000 = \$500{,}000$$

It is far better to have the insurance company agree up front that you have based your replacement cost reasonably. The company will agree not to impose a coinsurance clause—a penalty—in the event a loss occurs, even though you may not have given the right value. This is akin to adjusting the loss before it happens. A waiver of the coinsurance clause can be arranged by adding an agreed- or stipulated-amount endorsement to the policy.

Building Code Endorsement

The replacement cost, noted above, can be less than complete coverage.

- Building code endorsement: This addition to all property policies excludes building code requirements that were enacted after the building was built—for example, sprinklers, tempered glass and ramps and bathroom facilities for the handicapped.

If this endorsement is part of a policy, you can either have it removed or purchase additional coverage to protect against such an increase in value.

Difference in Conditions

Difference in conditions is a term that applies to insurance policies written to cover catastrophic property risk. For example, earthquake and flood coverage may be purchased in a difference in conditions package—a separate package—when it is not covered in a basic all-risks policy.

Pollution Hazards

Pollution hazards can be grouped as follows:

- Underground or airborne: Coverage is currently available for the cost of any government-mandated pollution cleanup.
- Asbestos: Coverage is available if you wish either (a) to leave or (b) to remove asbestos from a building.

Core Concepts

- ✓ Bodily injury, personal injury, property damage
- ✓ Commercial general liability
- ✓ Umbrella excess liability
- ✓ Automobile

LIABILITY INSURANCE

Liability insurance is a third-party bodily injury and property damage insurance. It covers you for claims made by others for their losses as a result of something you do or someone does on your behalf. To an attorney, bodily injury includes personal injury, but in the insurance vernacular, these are two different things.

In general, liability insurance covers:

- Bodily injury: Physical injury to a third party—the claimant. Along with the obvious injuries a person may suffer, it can be expanded to include mental anguish.
- Personal injury: This is a nonstandard coverage. Personal injury is usually defined in broad categories and written

on a named-peril basis. It covers certain types of injury, including:

—Slander
—Libel
—Unlawful detention
—Wrongful eviction. (You are covered if, for example, you placed a padlock on the tenant's door when he was away and he now cannot enter the premises. But if wrongful eviction emanates from a contractual dispute—for example, when a tenant leaves because you failed to do something under the lease—you are not covered.)

- Property damage: Such damage is defined as direct damage to physical property and loss of use thereof. For example, you will be covered if in the course of remodeling your center you cause the foundation of a nearby building to move. However, the construction of a building that blocks the view from your building is not a property damage claim.

Types of Liability Insurance Policies

- Commercial general liability. A very broad form of insurance that gives you bodily injury, personal injury and property damage coverage. It covers all your operations and automatically picks up any new operations.
- Umbrella excess liability: A vehicle for buying excess high limits of coverage. It is used as protection against catastrophic losses. It is usually with an aggregate limit, which means that if you have three centers and, for example, a $50 million umbrella policy, $50 million is all that the policy will pay. If you have a major loss, say a roof collapse

in one center that uses up the $50 million, your other centers will be unprotected because all the limits would have been absorbed. Umbrella policies can be bought on a per-location basis.

- Automobile nonownership coverage and hired car automobile liability: These policies do not extend coverage to the employee but do protect the owner of the policy. For example, if an employee driving his or her own vehicle while on the center's business has an accident, you are automatically covered under that employee's auto policy. However, if he or she carries low liability, the person suing that employee will sue you as well on the basis of agency—that the employee was doing something in the course of his or her employment. Auto nonownership and hired car auto liability assure you that the liability package you have structured to protect your assets picks up that exposure.
- Directors and officers liability: This coverage is used in a corporate setting. In a suit brought by stockholders or the public, this vehicle protects a company's directors and officers against mistakes and errors in judgment they may have made.
- Errors and omissions (E & O) coverage: E & O refers to liability arising out of errors or omissions in the performance of professional services. For example, a tenant stops paying rent and says you lied to him or misled him about the center's anchor or traffic. He claims that was why he went broke. When you sue to collect rent due, he might make a claim against you or a cross-complaint based upon this contention. Errors and omissions insurance covers you for this type of exposure. Historically, coverage has not been available for management of owned properties.

This is changing, however, and market availability of protection in this area should be regularly researched.

- Employment practices liability insurance: This protects the insured from employee generated claims for sexual harassment, discrimination, wrongful termination, etc.

Core Concepts

- ✓ Requirement under state law
- ✓ Ratings
- ✓ Dividends

WORKERS' COMPENSATION

Workers' compensation is a social insurance. The concept is that the employee is entitled to complete medical care and replacement of at least part of his or her wages if he or she is injured on the job. It does not matter whether he or she is at fault. In exchange for receiving this benefit, the employee gives up the right to sue the employer, claiming that employer's negligence.

Workers' compensation carries the following insuring agreements:

- It supplies coverage for the state compensation act and all the benefits of the state act.
- It provides employer's liability should the employee sue

and circumvent the exclusivity of the state compensation act.

In order to know what you have in terms of limits of protection, your employer's liability limit should be incorporated into your overall umbrella program. Remember that a commercial general liability policy excludes suits brought by employees.

Insurance Ratings

Employers have their own individual insurance ratings that are based on the workers' compensation losses that they as individual risks incur. A regulating authority publishes these rates. They annually update the rates based on loss reserves. (A reserve is the insurance carrier's best guess of what a particular claim will ultimately cost.)

You should review open reserve claims before they are incorporated into your rate makeup.

Dividends

Frequently, in the compensation field companies compete for your business on the basis of returning a portion of the premium in the form of dividends. Make sure that any dividend promises are based on some historical fact and realistic future projections.

Core Concepts

- ✓ Equipment failure
- ✓ Business interruption loss
- ✓ Bodily injury and property damage

BOILER AND MACHINERY INSURANCE

This kind of insurance was designed because steam boilers are historically excluded from fire insurance policies.

Much of the premium for this kind of coverage is based on the inspection service that the insurance company provides. Generally, the policy covers:

- Boiler explosion
- Machinery breakdown—sudden and accidental breakdown, not wear and tear
- Business interruption caused by breakdown of machinery
- Bodily injury and property damage resulting from covered incidents.

Core Concepts

✓ Employee theft

✓ Bonding employees

EMPLOYEE FIDELITY

"Employee theft insurance" best describes a fidelity bond. It covers monetary loss to the employer caused by the dishonest act of an employee. In the event of a loss, the burden of proof is always on the insured. Among the requirements:

- The employer has to do the accounting work to prove the loss occurred and how it occurred.
- The employer doesn't have to prove which specific employee did the deed.
- The employer has to prove to the bonding company that with this type of loss the only logical presumption is that the property was taken by an employee.
- The employer should know that inventory shortages are

not covered unless the person is caught in the act of stealing or has confessed to the act.

- The employer, not the bonding company, takes the risk if you have knowledge that a person has committed a dishonest act either while he has been employed by you or sometime in his past and you hired him with that knowledge.

Core Concepts

- ✓ Construction work; tenant and landlord
- ✓ Protects from subcontractors not paid
- ✓ Liquidated damages not necessarily included

SURETY BONDS

Surety bonds are issued by insurance companies. They are payment and performance bonds and are usually used on significant construction jobs. These bonds generally guarantee the following:

- That work will be completed per plans and specifications
- That you will pay no more than the agreed-upon price in the contract
- That all materials men—suppliers to the project—will be paid for their work.

Timeliness

Surety bonds do not guarantee timeliness. One way to guarantee that a job will be finished on time is to include liquidated damages, a penalty that says if a contractor doesn't complete the job by a certain date, he will pay a specified amount for every day the job is not completed. A bond guarantees payment of this penalty. In fairness, an incentive payment is usually given when a project comes in ahead of schedule.

Core Concepts

- ✓ Indemnity agreements
- ✓ Subrogation
- ✓ Certificate of insurance
- ✓ Landlord's vs. tenant responsibilities

THE LEASE DOCUMENT

Leases should spell out *who* is carrying *what* insurance. Determining in advance who is responsible for specific property and liability exposures avoids confusion, overlapping coverage and costly litigation to sort out responsibility after a loss occurs.

In addition to leases, there should be an awareness of any Reciprocal Easement Agreements or Joint Operating Agreements. These arise when a major department store owns its own realty (Building and/or Parking Area) and may present different areas of insurance responsibility.

Hold-Harmless Agreements

Risk transfer through well-drawn indemnity agreements, sometimes referred to as hold-harmless agreements, represents the first time of defense for the center landlord.

The types of hold-harmless agreements are:

- Basic agreement: Party A holds party B harmless for losses emanating from A's negligent acts.
- Intermediate agreement: Party A holds party B harmless for A's negligence and claims for which they are jointly negligent.
- Sole negligence agreement: Party A holds party B harmless for all losses, including those arising out of B's sole negligence. Such clauses may not be enforceable in certain jurisdictions. Consult an attorney.

Claimants will name shopping center landlords for everything that happens on a leased premises. To preclude this, landlords want tenants to hold them harmless for any claims arising out of that particular location, regardless of who is responsible. The sole negligence agreement flowing from the tenant (party A) to the landlord (party B):

- Relieves the landlord of responsibility for tenants' personal property, regardless of "fault"
- Avoids duplication of insurance coverages
- Clearly places responsibility for protecting the tenants' property on the tenants.

Waiver of Subrogation

Subrogation is the right that an insurance company has, if it pays a loss on your behalf, to go after any responsible third party. Most insurance policies permit you to waive this right prior to the occurrence of a loss.

Waivers of subrogation can be either unilateral or joint. The clause is of greater benefit to a tenant than to a landlord. Suppose, for example, you are a tenant and you cause a fire in the shopping center. If you have not gotten a subrogation waiver, the center landlord's insurance company is going to pay him and then come back and sue you. Without the subrogation waiver, you would have to buy fire legal liability coverage in order to protect yourself. With the subrogation waiver that cost can be saved.

Some landlords include a subrogation waiver as part of lease negotiations rather than as an automatic lease provision.

If you are asked by a tenant to include a joint waiver in your lease, make sure:

- That your policies permit it.
- That any policy issued to cover tenants' property waives subrogation against the landlord.
- That waiver is restricted only to losses that you can collect from your insurer.

Certificates

A certificate of insurance is an evidentiary piece of paper. As such:

- It is issued by the insurance carrier or by an insurance agent or broker.
- It spells out the amount and type of insurance.

- It is evidence that a policy is in effect and has the proper endorsements.
- It neither changes nor modifies the policy.

Landlord's Responsibility

The responsibility of the landlord under the lease is to protect, in the common area (unleased space shared by all tenants), all of the tenants against loss caused by the landlord's failure to maintain the common area. For example, the landlord has the responsibility to cover damages in the parking lot if someone trips and falls on a crack, as well as responsibility for assault cases.

There is a section in the lease that defines the landlord's insurance responsibility. Basically, it sets the items for which the tenant has to pay, and includes:

- The definition of the landlord's insurance, which will be billed in the CAM (common area maintenance) charge. It should be broad enough to allow pass-through of total premiums.
- The cost of all necessary insurance, from the landlord's perspective, to protect the center
- Working sufficiently inclusive to permit the landlord to carry adequate liability limits and to purchase coverage for catastrophic perils.

Tenant's Responsibility

Any operations of a tenant, whether on the leased premises or in the common area, are the responsibility of the tenant.

- Tenant liability insurance coverage includes:

  —Bodily injury, personal injury and property damage
  —Assumption, specifically, of liability via your indemnity agreement
  —Primary coverage as respects any carried by the landlord
  —The landlord named as an additional insured
  —Product liability
  —Owned, nonowned and hired automobile insurance
  —Evidence of workers' compensation coverage with employer's liability.

- Property insurance policies carried by a tenant should:

  —Be written on an "all risks of physical loss" basis
  —Be on a replacement cost basis
  —Include a subrogation waiver in the landlord's favor.

- Tenant's property insurance should cover:

  —Tenant's stock and equipment
  —Tenant's improvements. It is common for tenants to spend thousands of dollars on permanent improvements. Sooner or later the ownership of that property will revert to the shopping center landlord, so you have a vested interest in protecting that property. This coverage should name the landlord as an additional insured and loss payee. This means that if there is a loss payable, the insurance company must put the center landlord's name on the loss draft and obtain his signature before the draft can be cashed.
  —Glass, if it represents sufficient value in relation to the financial strength of the tenant
  —Boiler, pressure vessels or air-conditioning equipment, if it provides exclusive service to the tenant's premises.

- Insurance policies carried by a tenant should be from insurance companies acceptable to the landlord. Minimum ratings by A.M. Best Co., the recognized financial analyst in the insurance industry, are frequently inserted in the lease form.
- Each policy shall not be canceled or undergo any coverage change without 60 days' prior written notice being given the landlord.

Core Concepts

- ✓ Builder's risk
- ✓ Requirements of contractor

CONSTRUCTION CONTRACTS

If you undertake construction projects that will significantly add value to the property, these additions may not be covered under your existing policy. However, they can be insured with a course of construction property policy, which can be bought either by the contractor or by the shopping center landlord. Such policies are referred to as Builder's Risk Policies or Installation Floaters.

Landlord's Responsibility

It is the landlord's responsibility to pay for bonds if he requires them. (See the section on Surety Bonds above.)

Contractor's Responsibility

Among the contractor's many responsibilities are:

- Filing a certificate of liability and workers' compensation coverage. (This should be done before the contractor sets foot on your premises.)
- Adding the landlord as additional insured
- Specifying that the contractor's coverage is primary. This is important because when two policies are in effect, covering the same liability exposure, they will share the loss on a relative basis according to what their limits are. The landlord will be carrying much higher limits than the contractor, so if the landlord is brought in, his policy will pick up the lion's share of the loss.

Core Concepts

✓ Treat as contractor

✓ Consider special coverage

✓ Require certificates of insurance in advance

SPECIAL EVENTS—PUBLIC AREAS

From time to time, every center holds special events. From the standpoint of insurance, consider the following items:

- Lead time: Warn whoever works with you on your insurance so that he or she can investigate the type of coverage needed.
- Adequate coverage: Be sure that the people who are doing the event are offering the right amount of coverage.
- Special coverage: Get any that is needed. If, for example, the event involves high-value property—a jewelry display or automobiles or boats—you want to be sure you are protected should it be damaged.

- Hold-harmless agreements and insurance certificates: Require these in advance of the event from any group using the center.

Core Concepts

- ✓ Claims
- ✓ Reporting
- ✓ What to do after an occurrence

EFFECTIVE CLAIMS REPORTING

An insurance policy is a promise to pay if some future event occurs. That event is called a claim.

Claims Manual

It's essential that you have plans for handling all types of claims. A claims manual gives you the information you need all in one spot. To write the manual, a shopping center manager can get expert help from his or her insurance adviser. The manual need not be elaborate. It should be a working, day-to-day, flexible document that tells you who does what in the event of an occurrence. For example, major fires tend to occur in the middle of the night, and you have to know who is responsible to get someone to the center to board up the store or do any necessary salvage work.

Property Claims

Among the considerations to keep in mind:

- Protect property by being aware of possible causes of claims. For example: If a puddle is spotted in the public areas, post someone at the spot until it can be mopped up.
- Report claims promptly.
- Make a written report—write it at the time the loss occurs. Get as complete a record as you can concerning what happened.
- Get the names of all witnesses.

Liability Claims

Among the considerations to keep in mind:

- Take care of the injured party.
- Do not admit liability.
- Take pictures of the scene.
- Report the claim.
- Include pertinent lease information, as well as other particulars, in the written report.
- Defense is up to the carrier.

Workers' Compensation

Among the considerations to keep in mind:

- Take care of the injured employee.

- File the "Employer's First Report" required by your state.
- Maintain employee contact. When a person is injured you should keep in touch to express concern and to learn when and if he or she will be coming back to work.

Core Concepts

✓ Prepare a plan
✓ Provide training

A CATASTROPHE PLAN

A catastrophe plan sets out what everyone at the center is supposed to do in the event of a catastrophe, such as an earthquake or a bomb explosion. Among the points to consider for catastrophe planning:

- Give center's workers catastrophe training.
- Have the written plan easily accessible.

Core Concepts

✓ Insurers vs. insureds
✓ Brokers
✓ Evaluate services, not just premium

SELECTING A PROFESSIONAL

Insurance is sold by:

- Brokers: Persons licensed to represent insureds rather than insurance companies (insurers).
- Independent agents: Persons licensed to represent carriers. They may represent several.
- Direct writing companies: Companies having salespeople who represent only that one company.

Evaluating Prospects

Select a professional, not a premium. Don't select someone simply because he or she offers a policy with the cheapest premium. Remember, rates are subject to change, and long-term cost stability is important.

Interview prospects at your office. Look for someone whose credentials include:

- An understanding of your industry and a knowledge of what the problems in the shopping center industry are
- An understanding of the insurance industry
- Other clients in the shopping center industry.

Evaluate the services that prospects offer, then ask yourself the following:

- Do they have a full-time loss-control person who is readily accessible? One who will work with you and be part of your team?
- Do they have a full-time claims person who will be dedicated to your account, someone you can work with constantly?
- How do they work internally? Will one person be assigned to your account or will you be working with a team?

Core Concepts

- ✓ Premiums pay losses
- ✓ Capital influences markets
- ✓ Protect from catastrophic loss

HOW THE INSURANCE INDUSTRY WORKS

An insurance company does not have a magic formula to make money. It takes in premiums to pay losses. For every premium dollar an insurance company takes in, it can pay back 60 cents.

Why Coverage Availability Varies

There are insurance cycles within the industry that have very little to do with any other economic cycles. They tend to be competitive cycles because the insurance industry is dependent upon capital. Insurance companies are like banks: If they do not have surplus cash, they cannot write premiums. They are regulated on the ratio of premiums to surplus.

When capital leaves the industry and the available surplus shrinks, the companies are faced with a dilemma. If they don't build their surplus, they cannot write any more insurance. If they try to build their surplus by raising rates, they cannot find customers willing to buy the coverage. In both cases, the nature of the market changes, and coverage becomes more limited and more expensive.

How to Look at Your Insurance

Insurance is not a magic way to get rid of claims. Basically, all those costs come back to you, so it is unwise to look at insurance policies as a way to be reimbursed.

Look at all losses that occur in your center, with the exception of a catastrophic loss, as being an operating cost. The purpose of insurance is to protect you and to level the playing field so that if you get hit by a catastrophic loss you do not get wiped out.

Core Concepts

- ✓ Minimize risk
- ✓ Share risk

CONCLUSION

Risk is the chance you take of incurring a loss, and insurance is one method you can use to share that risk. It is the concern of risk management to protect a business against the possibility of accidental loss. The best way to do this is to avoid risk in the first place, but the next best way is to minimize your risks.

Minimizing risk is possible through noninsurance (by means of contracts that make others liable) or a professional insurance carrier. The specific sections of an insurance policy set up the terms and conditions that are to be included, whether the policy involves liability, property, workers' compensation or any of a number of other options. The lease spells out who carries what insurance, and it determines responsibility for specific property and liability in advance. Additional coverage may be required to cover either party for special projects, events and specific claims. When seeking someone to handle your insurance needs, be sure to interview prospects with a view to selecting a professional who is knowledgeable about your industry and can tend to your needs.

Glossary

The glossary that follows is a listing of key definitions compiled from this outline, with several terms not defined in the outline added for your information. The terms are defined within the context of this shopping center management topic.

Act of God An event that is caused by the forces of nature; one that humans could not have prevented by reasonable effort, e.g., an earthquake.

Actual cash value The cost, with a deduction for depreciation, of restoring or replacing destroyed property with property of similar like and quality. Usually defined as replacement cost less actual physical depreciation.

Additional insured An additional person or entity, other than the person covered by the policy, who has certain rights and coverages under the policy.

Agent A person licensed to represent one or several insurance companies.

All risk or special causes of loss insurance Insurance covering loss from all perils and causes unless specifically excluded in the policy. It is broader than a specified perils policy, which covers only those causes of loss enumerated in the policy.

Automobile nonownership coverage and hired car automobile liability Excess liability protection for the policyholder against accidents caused by others operating their own (or hired) vehicles on the holder's behalf.

Best Co. ratings The A.M. Best Company quantitatively and qualitatively evaluates the financial condition of insurance carriers. Its ratings reflect company management with an alphabetical rating ranging from A+ down to C. These letters are followed by a financial numerical rating, which reflects the size of the carrier's surplus (equity).

Bodily injury Part of general liability coverage that insures the policyholder against physical injury, including bodily injury, sickness, disease or death to a third party.

Boiler and machinery insurance Coverage for damage caused by or to boilers and machinery, including business interruption caused by boiler explosion or machinery breakdown.

Broker A licensed insurance professional who represents and acts on behalf of clients rather than an insurance company.

Building code endorsement An addition to property policies that includes coverage for work that might have to be done to comply with building code requirements enacted after the building was constructed.

Business income insurance Covers loss of net income, other than loss of rents, that would have been earned, including expenses incurred to reduce that loss.

Captive insurer An insurance company that is sponsored or owned by another entity whose primary purpose is to insure the exposures of its founders.

Carrier An insurance company.

Catastrophe An extreme loss due to an extreme happening such as a hurricane, earthquake or flood.

Certificate of insurance Document that verifies the type and amounts of insurance carried by policyholder.

Claim A demand to recover payment under an insurance policy; the amount of the loss.

Commercial general liability policy A broad form of third-party insurance that covers the policyholder in the event of bodily injury, personal injury and property damage claims.

Coinsurance clause A clause penalizing the insured if the amount insured for is less than a pre-agreed specified percentage of the value of the property insured.

Conditions The part of a policy that lays down the policy's ground rules—for example, how the policy is audited and to whom you should present a claim.

Coverage The extent of the insurance provided by a policy.

Declaration The "housekeeping" page on the front of a policy that identifies the policyholder, policy dates and type and limits of coverage.

Deductible The portion of first dollar loss assumed by the insured.

Definitions The section of an insurance policy that defines the terms used in the policy.

Difference in conditions A separate insurance package written to cover catastrophic property exposures.

Direct writing company An insurance company whose sales force represents only that one company.

Directors and officers liability Protects a company's directors and officers in the event of a suit brought by stockholders or the public for negligence in the performance of their responsibilities.

Endorsement A written addition to a policy.

Errors and omissions coverage Protects against liability arising out of errors and omissions in the performance of professional services.

Exclusion A provision of a policy identifying those things not covered by that policy.

Fidelity bond Employee theft insurance covering monetary loss to the employer caused by a dishonest act of an employee.

Hired car automobile liability Provides contingent coverage for short-term rental vehicles.

Hold-harmless agreement An indemnity agreement in which one party's legal liability for damages is assumed by the other party to the contract. It protects one against losses from someone else's failure to fulfill an obligation.

Indemnity agreements See Hold-harmless agreement.

Insurance A contract between a risk-taker (the insurer) and another party (the insured) in which, for a fee (the premium), the insurer agrees to pay the insured for losses to something specific (the risk) due to named causes (hazards or perils). The insurer may also assume the obligation to pay a third party (the claimant) on behalf of the insured.

Insuring agreement The section of an insurance policy that states what the policy covers.

Liability Usually a financial obligation and the cost of meeting it.

Liability insurance See Commercial general liability policy.

Liability limit In the event of a loss, the maximum amount the insurer is required to pay.

Loss The injury or damage sustained by the insured; in liability policies, it means the payments made by the insurer on behalf of the insured.

Named insured Person or business entity designated on a policy as being insured.

Named-peril insurance Coverage that specifies the perils that it covers.

Occurrence Broadens the definition of an "accident" to include incidents that occur over a period of time.

Perils Inherent things, such as windstorms or explosions, that can cause a loss or injury.

Personal injury A nonstandard part of liability coverage insuring the policyholder, on a named-perils basis, against such things as libel, slander, unlawful detention, etc.

Policy The written insurance contract.

Policyholder The person or company having an insurance contract.

Premium The amount paid for an insurance policy.

Property damage Part of liability coverage defined as direct damage to physical property and loss of use thereof.

Property insurance First-party insurance covering the insured for damage to his or her personal or real property or the loss of its use.

Replacement cost Today's cost of construction, without considering depreciation.

Risk The peril insured against; the chance of loss.

Risk management The branch of management that is concerned with protecting a business against the risks of accidental loss.

Risk Retention Act companies This 1986 federal act permitted industries to jointly set up insurance vehicles that were licensed in a single state and then to write business in other states.

Subrogation The right of an insurance company to recover its loss from the responsible party after paying the policyholder's claim.

Surety bonds Payment and performance bonds usually used on significant construction jobs.

Third-party insurance It protects the insured against liability arising out of property or bodily damage to others caused by another party.

Umbrella excess liability Form of insurance that protects against losses in excess of amounts covered by other liability insurance policies. It is used to protect against catastrophic losses.

Waiver The surrender of a right that is legally yours.

Warranty A statement that conditions will exist during the policy term and if found untrue, or not in existence, would invalidate the policy.

Workmen's compensation See Workers' compensation.

Workers' compensation A social insurance that entitles an employee to medical care and replacement of at least part of his or her wages if he or she is injured on the job. In return for this the employee gives up the right to sue his or her employer. Claims are generally paid by private insurers, but the rates are set by state boards.